THE HISTORY OF SWITZERLAND

*A Fascinating Guide
to this Wonderful Country in Central Europe*

ANDREW GREEN

TABLE OF CONTENTS

What's so great about Switzerland?

Well, the flag is a plus.

INTRODUCTION

Mountains. Neutrality. Watches. Secret bank accounts. Cheese and chocolate. In the modern world, these seem to be the things we think of when discussing the country of Switzerland. We love its products and dream of visiting its dramatic Alpine playgrounds. Of course, there is more to this small nation than a vacation spot or a political stance, but a surprising amount of Switzerland's fortunes (both monetary and otherwise) have been determined by its location. The natural barriers of two formidable mountain ranges, and its location in the figurative center of Europe, have always set Switzerland apart, and that separation has produced its unusual status throughout its history and into the era of the modern world.

Switzerland's population does not reach 9 million people, and on a list of the world's 194 countries and dependent territories, Switzerland is 132nd, followed in large part by protectorates and island countries. Yet modern Switzerland is a hub of world activity and a leader in economics and human development. Its cities are consistently lauded for their high quality of life – though such quality comes at a price, with some of the highest costs of living in the world. Switzerland boasts the highest nominal wealth per adult, and the world's eighth-highest gross domestic product. Swiss citizenship is a much sought-after status. Swiss men and women have the longest life expectancies in the world. How did such a small and cut-off land become so central (and not just in its location) to the events of the western world?

In this history, we'll look at the forces that formed this powerful and influential country.

GEOGRAPHY

Switzerland lies landlocked in the center of Western Europe. To the south is Italy, to the west, France. Germany is to the north and Lichtenstein and Austria are to the East. The little country is extremely mountainous, its geography divided between the great mass of the Swiss Alps, which spans the entire southern half of the country, and the Jura range, a sub-alpine mountain range that lies along the border between Switzerland and France. Between these two natural barriers is the Swiss Plateau, which lies east-to-west on relatively flat ground. Most of the country's 8.5 million population resides on the Swiss Plateau, where the country's major metropolises (Bern, Zurich, Lucerne, and Lausanne) are situated. This is not to say that the spectacular mountains go unpopulated; they are peppered with high-altitude cities, tourism, and industry. Today Switzerland is composed of 26 administrative cantons, and many of which have been in existence since before the Middle Ages.

Early History of Switzerland

Prehistory

The presence of humans in the area that would become Switzerland can be dated to 150,000 years ago. Farming settlements dating from 6000 to 5000 BC have been found at Gächlingen, a municipality that still exists in the far north of the country on the Danube River. Afterward, as was the case with most of Central Europe, the Hallstatt culture populated the area through the Bronze Age (from approximately the 12th to 6th centuries BC) followed by the Iron Age culture of La Tène (450 BC to the 1st Century BC - the Roman Conquest).

In 15 BC, Roman brothers Tiberius (a future emperor) and Drusus conquered the Alps, making them part of the Roman Empire. The region was divided into two Roman provinces, Gallia Belgica (later called Germania Superior) and Raetia. The first Roman settlement on the Rhine, Augusta Raurica, had appeared by 44 BC. Augusta Raurica and several other towns grew quite large and prosperous in the first two centuries AD; the remainder of the surrounding plateau was largely utilized for agricultural estates. Today, Augusta Raurica is an important excavation site, where the remains of an amphitheater, aqueducts, town walls, a theater and a town forum with temples and an assembly chamber have been uncovered.

By the end of the 4th Century AD, despite its efforts to defend the territory, the Roman Empire was driven out of the area by increasing attacks from Germanic tribes, which then settled into the abandoned plateau.

Through the 4th Century the Swiss plateau and the Alps were divided between Alemannia and Burgundy, and finally the entire region was taken into the Frankish Empire when it defeated Alemannia and overtook the Burgundians. Thus, it remained for the next three centuries, until the Frankish Empire was divided in Charlemagne's Treaty of Verdun in 843AD, renaming the region into Middle Francia and East Francia. The two regions were reunited by the Holy Roman Empire sometime around 1000 AD. This led to various kingdoms controlling the area – houses such as Savoy, Zähringer, Kyburg and Habsburg, with the ambitious land-grabbing clan of Habsburgs annexing more and more of the land under their rulership.

In fact, Switzerland was the first Habsburg territory in the Holy Roman Empire and even is home to the Habsburgs original castle, Hawk Castle, or Habichtsburg Castle (1020 AD).

GEOGRAPHIC ADVANTAGE

Despite being a part of the Holy Roman Empire, the area that would one day become Switzerland enjoyed a certain autonomous privilege simply because of geographical isolation. With difficult mountain ranges both in the north and south of the territory, the cantons were too inconveniently located for any heavy-handed rulership.

Under the rule of the Holy Roman Empire, Switzerland's cantons were subject to "imperial immediacy," that is to say, they were "immediately" under the authority of the Holy Roman Emperor without the go-between of a duke or other intermediary. Theoretically this status was not to be coveted. For many territories, immediacy resulted in rather high expectations and demands being placed on a territory by the emperor, and without an intermediary, there was no effective way to compromise.

However, should the Holy Roman Emperor choose to focus attention elsewhere, the countries with imperial immediacy found themselves able and expected to exercise their own imperial powers, giving them a pleasing amount of autonomy. This was the case with Switzerland – it was simply out of reach, difficult to control, and had nothing of sufficient value to warrant the trouble required. The Holy

Roman Emperor had far bigger fish to fry, and Switzerland was left alone.

For centuries, then, Switzerland's communities were mostly left to themselves to govern their own affairs. The people of the region became quickly accustomed to these freedoms and developed a fierce sense of protectiveness for their lands. The climate and terrain, rough as it was, in combination with this protectiveness, produced generations of hardy, daring and well-trained fighters ready to defend themselves and their small, resilient homelands.

THE GOTTHARD PASS

The landscape of Swiss inaccessibility was changed by the completion of the Gotthard Pass. 13th Century Switzerland, through pasteurizing herds of cattle, enjoyed an unusual level of prosperity in its production of dairy products, and was eager to promote trade with Italy, which lay south of the most forbidding range of the Alps. The Gotthard Pass was the extension of an ancient local route located on the lowest point between the Alpine summits of Pizzo Lucendro and Pizzo Centrale. Still, the road afforded no real advantage until the completion of a wooden bridge that crossed the Schollenen Gorge, which had previously been inaccessible in springtime due to the violent rush of snowmelt waters. The Gotthard Pass extended from just south of Lake Lucerne, then wound southward through the Alps to emerge near Bellinzona, not far from the Italian border and only 108 km from Milan.

Now travelers could take the Gotthard Pass to its summit of almost 7000 feet and then travel directly south toward prosperous Duchy of Milan. For centuries afterward, Gotthard Pass remained the only feasible way through the Alps to Italy. Thus, beginning in the mid-13th Century, the Gotthard Pass opened trade between Switzerland and Italy. But more importantly, the opening of the pass created a far shorter route from Germany to Italy, and in fact, established a new trade route between all northern and southern Europe. Suddenly, Switzerland became an extremely important piece of land.

THE SWISS CONFEDERACY RESPONDS TO HABSBURG INTERFERENCE

Now the Holy Roman Empire, led by Rudolf I of the Habsburgs, took notice of the potential wealth and advantages of Switzerland. In 1291, Rudolf I stepped in and took control of the important area of Lucerne by purchasing it from Murbach Abbey, the Benedictine monastery around which the village had grown.

In response, three of Switzerland's nearby rural cantons bordering Lake Lucerne, Uri, Schwyz and Unterwalden (sometimes called the "Forest Cantons"), made formalized agreements between themselves regarding mountain trade routes and other common interests. Uri, at the time, held the territory of the Gotthard Pass. The trio formed the Schweizerische, or the Swiss Confederation.

These three cantons had long been rivals, as likely to fight one another as join forces, so this was not the first time that the question or treaties or agreements had been approached. But now, the urgency of the situation, as outsiders took control from them, prompted more effort for the cantons to make this agreement work.

The Federal Charter of 1291 is considered the founding document of the Old Swiss Confederacy. Over the next 100 years, further Swiss cantons joined this Confederacy, with the end of both the 14th and 15th centuries seeing dramatic increases in the Confederacy's size.

From this point forward, the Swiss people, accustomed to their autonomy, reacted violently to any attempts to encroach upon their country. The wars for Switzerland's independence continued for centuries, from small insurrections to large battles. Witnesses surviving these fights went home to spread tales of the fearsomeness of Swiss warriors.

The Warriors of Switzerland

Origins

The rugged landscape of Switzerland, the wildlife (including wolves and bears), and their own determination to maintain independence gave the Swiss people a predisposition toward skillful fighting and self-defense. They developed significant martial skills. What's more, centuries of self-reliance had turned them into a people who demanded their freedom and would settle for nothing less; their obvious pride and ferocity on the battlefield made them the terror of Europe. There were a few decisive battles that established and furthered this status.

In 1315, at the Pass of Morgarten, fighters from Schwyz faced down an Austrian army. Schwyz had struck against the Holy Roman Empire by plundering a monastery, which of course prompted a military response, and Austria sent 9000 troops, including 2000 mounted knights. Mounted knights were, at the time, the height of military expertise and power. The Austrian force came under the command of Holy Roman Emperor Leopold I.

Schwyz was aware of the Austrians' approach. They had only 1300 men in their force, so the people retreated behind a series of manmade earthworks and wooden palisades. Leopold chose to attack via the Pass at Morgarten, the weakest point of the series. The Austrian army approached in a column, with its vanguard of mounted knights in the lead. The vanguard found itself redirected by enemy defenses and then set upon by a small and stubborn group of fighters blocking the route. Abruptly the rest of the Austrian army was at a standstill, and exposed, out in the open.

Schwyz fighters then cut off the mounted vanguard from the rest of the army, again by blocking the road, and a second group rained stones down on the mounted knights and then flew at them with axes and halberds, driving them into the marshes and cut them down. Most of the 2000 casualties of the battle were Austrian mounted knights.

This relatively small victory for the Schwyz, thanks in part to clever use of the terrain and the element of surprise, sent shockwaves throughout the empires. The guerilla warfare tactics of the Swiss people were unheard of. The chivalry of mounted knights supported the belief that battles should be fought almost tournament-style, with a particular etiquette. It was apparent that these rough canton-dwellers had no respect for chivalry. The tales of fearsome Swiss foes spread throughout Europe.

In 1385, Habsburg emperor Leopold III attempted to expand his lands into Switzerland. Once more, war broke out. Leopold's army faced off against Swiss forces on July 9, 1386 north of Sempach (in the canton of Lucerne). The Austrians again were surprised by the swiftness of the Swiss attack. By rushing their attack forward, the Swiss forces sought to keep the Austrians on terrain unsuitable for mounted attacks. Indeed, the Austrian knights were forced to abandon their horses. Swiss halberdiers, wearing light armor compared to the heavily protected knights, took many casualties at first.

Historically, Swiss warriors are seldom deterred or demoralized by poor odds – in fact, the more the odds line against them, the harder they seem to fight. And to an enemy, what could be more terrifying than an opposing force willing to fight to the death? A stubborn, angry and determined bunch, the halberdiers regrouped and pressed their attack toward breaking through the line of Austrian pikemen. Once through the barrier, they proceeded to slaughter another 2000 Austrians, a considerable victory considering their own casualties of merely 200. The Austrians were driven back again, and again, stories spread throughout Europe of the terrifying Swiss halberdier.

The Pikemen's Square

In 1422 at the Battle of Arbedo, the resiliency of the Swiss halberdier found its limitations. Territorial disputes over Bellinzona (near the south end of the Gotthard pass) led to war between the Duchy of Milan and the Swiss cantons.

About 2,500 Swiss confederate soldiers marched on the city of Bellinzona. In response, the Milanese army sent 16,000 troops (including 5000 cavalrymen). The Milanese general launched a surprise attack upon the Swiss, who quickly made a square formation and defended themselves. Once more, the Swiss warriors were able to thwart cavalry attacks, and the Milanese soldiers were forced to dismount. But at this point, the Swiss were simply vastly outnumbered. The Milanese persistently assaulted the Swiss until, having suffered about 500 casualties, the Swiss elected to cut their losses and retreat. Theoretically, as the Swiss forces were made of warriors from multiple cantons without the same training or commanders, chaos would have been a predictable result of such dire circumstances. Yet with precision and likeminded purpose, the Swiss broke through the Milanese line and retreated into the mountains. Strong discipline was added to the many traits that European forces feared from a Swiss army.

The Swiss themselves, however, considered this defeat as a lesson. The halberd was insufficient as its army's standard weapon. The canton of Lucerne had joined the Confederacy in 1352, and in its capital city of Lucerne, a council was held to determine a solution. It was here that the Swiss decided to employ the use of long pikes and greatly increase the use of pikemen.

The long pike was unwieldly as a weapon, and in single combat was practically useless. To see it serve its purpose, it must be employed by a phalanx of men, each brandishing one of the long, sharp pikes as they all move in unison. The effective use of a pike phalanx requires a great deal of training and discipline, yet these seem to be the very traits in which Swiss warriors excelled.

In a standard Swiss pike phalanx, the men in the front four rows held their pikes at varying levels from ground to eye-level. The next four rows served two purposes: to replace pikemen lost in the front four, and to stand close enough together, with their pikes held vertically, to make a highly effective barrier against enemy arrows. By practicing this phalanx technique, Swiss pikemen formed a spiny, mobile barrier that could stop a cavalry attack dead in its tracks. Horses quite wisely refused to get anywhere near such a frightening deathtrap, and any knight who forced the way forward would find himself and his horse skewered.

That a defeat proved the value of these pike phalanxes is rather ironic, but even Swiss defeats had an air of purposefulness in them. In 1444, after the Treaty of Tours stopped the Hundred Years' War, the French king found himself with a mercenary army and nothing to do. He allied with Habsburg Emperor Friedrich III and sent

40,000 troops marching into the Swiss Confederacy, again in effort to expand territories. A reconnaissance force of 1500, which held 1200 Swiss warriors, was sent to block the army's path.

The two groups clashed at St. Jakob an der Birs, and the Swiss were clearly outnumbered once again; nevertheless, the stubborn and proud Swiss warriors insisted upon fighting; their commanders even ordered retreat and the warriors of the cantons refused. Up to the battle itself, retreat would have remained possible, and still, they threw themselves at these invaders to their lands. The Swiss fought to the last man, the battle ranging from weaponry and battlefield tactics until losses and confusion reduced the entire encounter to violent hand-to-hand combat. Even though they were defeated, the noteworthy fact was that Swiss pike formations held out for five hours against the superior forces, and the Swiss managed to kill approximately 4000 of the invading mercenary troops.

THE BURGUNDIAN WARS

In 1473, yet again, a foreign ruler wished to enlarge his territories by snatching up Swiss cantons. This time, it was the Duke of Burgundy, Charles the Bold, who made a play to declare himself a king by expanding his lands to Italy, which, of course, meant taking the Swiss Confederacy into his territory. This time it was not only the Confederacy he angered but the Austrians and Alsatians, who united with the Swiss to drive the Duke away with at the Battle of Hericourt.

Charles did not give up; in 1476 he pursued a plan to cut straight through the middle of the Swiss Confederacy by first taking Bern. On their march to Bern, the Burgundians encountered the small town of Grandson. The Duke's army crushed the small resistance there and killed many of their Swiss prisoners by hanging or drowning them, an act that naturally enraged the Swiss. Charles the Bold, living up to his name, apparently had chosen to ignore tales of the danger of an enraged Swiss soldier.

A few days later the bloodthirsty Swiss Confederacy met Charles' forces in the Battle of Grandson. They employed their square pike technique, not only as a battle strategy but as a diversion, occupying Charles' efforts, decimating his cavalry, and whittling away at his forces and ammunition while the major mass of the Swiss Confederacy's army approached from the northeast. His forces were already badly battered when Charles realized that he had not yet met the entirety of Swiss forces. He fled the battle with his attendants, leaving behind a considerable amount of treasure.

There were two more fights, and the Swiss won both: Morat 1476, and Nancy 1477 – at the latter, Charles the Bold was killed. His death marked the end of the Burgundian wars.

The pike block's effectiveness demonstrated that the mounted knight was now antiquated. By the end of the 15th Century, over two thirds of European infantries were armed with long pikes.

Swiss Mercenaries

Their victory in the Burgundian Wars left no doubts in the minds of European powers: Swiss fighters were a coveted asset. European monarchs began hiring Swiss mercenaries to supplement their forces and to act as bodyguards. It was commonly believed that having a Swiss contingent within your forces could make the difference between victory and defeat.

During the 15th Century, soldiering was sort of a part-time occupation to supplement the Swiss farmer's income; something for him to do while he waited for harvests. With the passage of time, the number of Swiss farms began to decrease as cattle herding required more and more land for grazing. As a result, soldiering became a rather common full-time occupation. They were known for carrying two weapons: a traditional Swiss halberd and a golden-handled longsword.

A Swiss warrior's reputation as loyal, reliable, and ferocious on the battlefield was no exaggeration. Even more, monarchs liked the impartiality of the Swiss. Because they were hired, and not the king's royal subjects, they weren't embroiled in political arguments or subject to disagreeable taxes or laws, and they were therefore fighting without grudges against their employer.

By 1481, about 6000 Swiss mercenaries worked in service of King Louis XI of France, and by 1497, 100 Swiss guards acted as the French king's personal guards, or his "Garde de Cent Suisses" (Guard of 100 Swiss). These men not only watched over the king in his palace, but also accompanied him into battle.

THE PAPAL SWISS GUARD

The popes of the Renaissance were far more like kings than they were religious figures, operating with the same sense of politics, arranging marriages, making alliances with nations, and leading forces into battle. For decades, popes had held alliances with the Confederacy and had used Swiss mercenaries in battles.

Pope Julius II was sixty years old but remained an energetic military leader who desired to be both the ruler of Italy and to increase his hold over European power through his papal office. In these pursuits, he wanted to ensure his safety with a cadre of personal bodyguards. The Swiss had the advantage of being unaligned with any European power. Julius had also seen the Swiss in battle personally. He was witness to their prowess when France warred with Naples in the Italian Wars, in addition to serving as the Bishop of Lausanne for a time that let him become well acquainted with the Swiss people.

Julius's Swiss advisor was a cleric named Peter von Hertenstein, who had long been in the service of the papal authority. When Julius inquired about the acquisition of Swiss bodyguards, Hertenstein agreed to assist, and even recommended a relative, Kaspar von Silenen, as commander.

In 1505, Julius sent Hertenstein to Swiss lands with instructions to employ 200 Swiss guards; this expensive venture was funded by the famously wealthy Fugger family of Germany, which controlled the European copper market and a major portion of the European economy in the 16th century.

Upon his arrival, Hertenstein found the Confederacy's government less willing to cooperate than he had hoped. Swiss mercenary service had entered a stage of controversy, with great concerns over the sheer numbers of Swiss men who were in the employ of foreign powers. Only five years before, an unfortunate battle had pitched two contingents of Swiss soldiers against each other – one in the service of Louis XII of France, the other in service of Ludovico il Moro of Milan -- resulting in many losses.

Another problem was that "papal guard duty" did not appeal to the warriors of the Confederacy. It sounded quite dull, to stand around guarding an old man, compared to the fun of fighting bloody fights for kings with the promise of booty.

For these reasons, only 150 Swiss troops went to Rome in the winter of 1505 with Kaspar von Silenen, the first captain of the Papal Swiss Guard. Pope Julius granted them the title of "Defenders of the Church's Freedom."

For the most part, Papal Swiss Guard duty is ceremonial. In May of 1527, however, Rome was sacked by mutinous troops of Charles V, the Holy Roman Emperor. Roman defenders, outnumbered, soon found the city walls breached. The militia retreated, and only 189 Swiss guards stayed at their posts in the Vatican, holding their ground the Campo Centro (the Vatican cemetery) and giving Pope Clement time to escape. The Swiss Guard cut down 900 enemy troops, losing 147 of their own as the remaining guards escaped with the Pope. The Papal Guard remains in service today, though through the centuries the size of the guard has changed and even, at times, been disbanded.

Requirements for serving in the Papal Swiss Guard are quite strict. Candidates must be men who are:

- » Citizens of Switzerland
- » Roman Catholic
- » Of good moral and ethical background
- » Between the ages of 19 and 30
- » At least 174 centimeters tall
- » In possession of a professional diploma or high school degree

» Swiss military trained.

If a candidate meets all these traits, he can apply to the guard's recruiting office in Neuhausen where he will undergo a rigorous interview process. Plans have been proposed to allow the inclusion of women in the Swiss Papal Guard, but such plans remain in the "ideas" phase and no implementation of the inclusion of women has started.

Successful applicants go to Rome, and at once are put into a training program. They learn the traditions, behavior, and the occasional oddities of papal service. They work out at a gym and study martial arts. Tradition dictates that they practice halberd drilling, but since the assassination attempt against Pope John Paul II in 1981, the Swiss Guard has also trained at a nearby Italian firing range to learn care and service of guns.

Purportedly, the most difficult part of the job is standing motionless in the Italian sun wearing over 50 pounds of traditional armor. The stoic guards master psychological tricks to handle the task.

Defeat of Emperor Maximilian

Further cantons joined over the Confederacy over the centuries, increasing its power and expanding its reach from the Jura Mountains in the north to the Alps in the south. The Confederacy determinedly battled the Holy Roman Empire until in 1499, they defeated Emperor Maximilian I in the Swabian War, a dispute over the control of the Val Mustair and the Umbrail Pass in the Grisons. The Grisons were not part of the Confederacy yet, but Swiss troops were obligated to the Grisons by contract. Through a series of victories over the Habsburg allies, the Swiss won, basically, the Confederacy's figurative independence – simply in the fact that, although the Confederacy was still considered a part of the Holy Roman Empire, that Empire would no longer try to interfere with them, lifting imperial taxes and jurisdiction. Further cantons joined the Confederacy shortly thereafter, and Switzerland's area rapidly expanded in the early 15th Century, with another surge in size at the 15th Century's end.

Reformation in the Cantons

During the 15th Century, Switzerland fought not only for its independence from the Holy Roman Empire but from excessive influence of the Church. Several monasteries had already been put under secular management. While, in general, teachers were still priests, the administration of schools was in the hands of the cantons, not the church. Still, the Swiss populace could see the vivid contrast between the luxuries enjoyed by the Church and its priests and note its marked contrast to the standard of living borne by the population's majority. It did not escape their notice, either, that many of those priests, far from supervision, lived hedonistic lives nothing like the rules that the Church dictated. When stirrings of reformation spread through Europe, many in the Swiss Confederacy were ready for a change.

HULDRYCH ZWINGLI

Huldrych Zwingli served as a priest in Einsiedeln. His studies were in the renaissance humanist tradition, which contrary to modern views of "humanism," is a specifically religious viewpoint that simply wants to revert to the classical traditions and dispense with intermediaries between man and God (that is, to reduce or even dispense with the need for the Church and its priests). Therefore, as early as 1516 he spoke out against the injustice of the Church's hierarchies.

He was eventually called to Zurich, where he became a well-known revolutionary protestant, adding to his fame by speaking out against corrupt political processes and condemning the mercenary business (already falling out of favor, as previously mentioned). In Zurich, Zwingli's ideas were well-received. His most historically famous stance against the Church took place in the "Affair of the Sausages," (1522) when Zwingli openly defended locals who ate meat during Lent, saying that the Bible never dictated when Christians should, or should not, fast, nor what they should eat during Lent. Of course, this caused backlash from the Church but too late − the damage was done, and Zwingli's popularity grew immensely. In 1523, Zurich's city council took Zwingli's reformatory plans seriously enough to convert to Protestantism.

Within two years, the reformation swept through Zurich. The church in Zurich became secularized, with the state taking control of Church properties as well as the social works previously mandated by the Church. Churches were stripped of their opulent decorations. Priests were paid by the state and relieved of celibacy; convents disbanded. By 1528, the cities of Basel, Bern, Bienne, Mulhouse, St. Gallen and Schaffhausen had all followed Zurich's example, converting to Protestantism.

The Catholic powers were not silent on the matter. Catholic cantons quickly took power over the priests, snapping their lax behaviors back into shape so that the public could no longer point at corrupt priests as a symbol of church decay. Both production and possession of printed materials of the Reformation were outlawed. The study of Hebrew and Greek were banned, which prevented independent Biblical study.

Zwingli's reformation differed from Martin Luther's on points that may seem somewhat impenetrable to outsiders; their major point of disagreement was on the nature of communion and whether bread and wine were the literal flesh and blood or Christ or merely symbols of them. Reformer, pastor and theologian John Calvin of Geneva stood in the middle of this debate, trying to find a middle ground that would appease both sides of the argument by emphasizing that the sacramental symbols have great meaning but not individual power.

John Calvin

Meanwhile, in Geneva, Calvin was generating controversy with his developing theology, including doctrines of predestination and the sovereignty of God. Originally interested in priesthood, he broke with the Catholic Church in 1530 and threw in with the Reformation, where his beliefs were more obviously supported. Calvin's viewpoint of religion was far stricter and more demanding than the kinder, gentler Protestantism of Zwingli, but ideologically they were united against the Roman Catholic Church. (Later in this history, we will see how John Calvin inadvertently changed the history not only of religion but of the Swiss watchmaking industry.)

Reformation in Zurich was accomplished quickly and was popular enough to cause alarm in many of the Roman Catholic cantons. At the time, the Confederacy consisted of thirteen cantons; those in Alpine territories remained fiercely Catholic. The reasoning was not solely religious; they also relied strongly on the monies generated by mercenary work (which the Reformation disapproved of strongly). As early as 1524, the Alpine cantons formed the League of the Five Cantons specifically to fight the spread of the Reformation. In response, the Protestant-reformed cities created their own alliance, that went by several names, but which was basically the Christian Confederation. From 1524 through 1529, skirmishes erupted between the two groups, but it was not until a Protestant pastor was burned at the stake in Schwyz in 1529 that

Zurich declared war on the League of the Five Cantons. The First and Second Wars of Kappel followed.

BATTLES, SPOKEN AND FOUGHT

Oddly enough, the First War of Kappel was staged, but unfought. Forces gathered from Catholic cantons with the intent of attacking Protestant cantons. Battle was avoided, though narrowly, when a resolution was reached without any bloodshed. The Second War of Kappel, however, brought over 7000 Catholic troops to attack Zurich. Zwingli's influence had caused the Protestant cantons to stop trading with Catholic cantons, and the embargo on food was pressing the issue, causing the Catholic cantons to physically move on Zurich. Zwingli, for himself, was eager to fight – unfortunately he was killed on the battlefield, thus halting the spread of his version of Protestantism to areas below the Rhine. The Catholics defeated the Protestants, and the Protestants were forced into a treaty.

The treaty demanded that the Protestant alliance dissolve. Catholicism was given priority in common territories, although most communities that had already converted to Protestantism could remain so. Reverting to Catholicism was enforced only in territories that were valuable trade route locations. Interestingly, cantons themselves were permitted to choose religions, so long as the Catholics maintained a majority in the diet (the governing body of the Confederacy).

Regardless of the treaty's terms, Catholic cantons did try on numerous fronts to bring protestant converts back into the fold with enticements rather than force. Their focus was on education and public works. The first Jesuit school was opened in Lucerne, with many others to follow, as well as a Catholic university for Swiss priests, a nunciature in Lucerne, and a Capuchin monk cloister, and a figurative military alliance with the Pope (which, being underfunded, had to operate in treaties rather than battles). In many cases, the resulting division of Catholics versus Protestants was resolved by simply having both groups represented in the cantons' individual governments.

With its own alliance dissolved, Zurich aligned itself with several southern German cities practicing Protestantism – however, when Germany went to war over religion, Zurich, along with other Swiss cantons, remained neutral.

Heinrich Bullinger, who succeeded Zwingli in Zurich, was a prolific writer and participant in the formalization of Protestantism, and he attempted to reconcile the two ideologies. In 1548, Bullinger assisted John Calvin in writing the *Consensus Tigurinus* (which attempted to resolve the schism between Protestants regarding communion). In 1566, Bullinger was instrumental in creating the two versions of the *Confessio Helvetica*, which expressed the commons beliefs of the Reformed Churches in Switzerland; the *Confessio* was adopted by many other protestant European regions.

This written work, along with the *Heidelberg Catechism* (1563) and the *Canons of Dordrecht* (1619) were the foundation of theology of Protestant Calvinism.

Swiss Population Growth and the Peasants' Uprisings

While it remained protected from the outside countries, Switzerland suffered divisions inside by both religious conflict and violent class struggles. The Swiss peasant wars rose out of a tax dispute, when the rural folk of Switzerland took offense at taxation from the noble classes.

Switzerland suffered many plague surges (or about 31 plague years) within the cantons from 1500 to 1640. Viciously deadly smallpox outbreaks were particularly brutal on child mortality rates in roughly five-year cycles after 1580. Yet overall, the population managed to grow during the 16th Century by about 35%, or from about 800,000 persons to approximately 1.1 million.

The rise in population had several consequences:

1. Increased dependance on imports

2. Increased prices

3. Generational settlements of estates in the countryside led to smaller and smaller properties owned by families, until

the land was insufficient to support those who lived on
it.

4. The number of day laborers increased (that is, men who
    would work a day at a time for a day's wages)

5. Rural areas became increasingly financially dependent on
    cities.

Political power, however, was held by a few rich families, and as
the 16th Century passed, these families began to see their roles as a
hereditary right. Predictably, these families became insular, forming
their own exclusive circles that allowed for no new voices to be heard.

Around 1525, dissention made itself known among the cantons,
either arguments, public statements or outright fights in which both
peasants the merchant-classes rebelled against this new order of
nobility and their demands for taxes from the people. The Swiss
people wanted a return to the old, common rights that the cantons
used to enjoy. This conflict continued for decades, with revolts
breaking out in various cantons and the uprising spreading from
region to region.

Finally, around 1650, when it seemed that the self-proclaimed
nobility planned to permanently ignore the population's demands,
peasants and working classes from numerous cantons united in the
Huttwil Treaty. Through this treaty, they declared themselves a
political entity that was independent from city authority, and that it

had full sovereignty in its territories over both political and military matters. Then, the peasant armies began to siege Bern and Lucerne.

The peasants were defeated by the cities' forces, and the Huttwil League was forcibly broken apart by an army from Zurich. Leaders of the insurrection were dealt with severely, many of them tortured, imprisoned or even executed.

Even so, ruling aristocrats were not foolish; they realized that they relied upon their people for production and taxes. Presumably following the torture, execution and other punishments, they instituted reforms, lowered taxes and appeased a number of the rebellion's demands. It is believed that this compromise prevented the complete absolutism that resulted in the French Revolution in Switzerland's neighboring country.

THE THIRTY YEARS' WAR

By the time the Thirty Years' War (1618 – 1648) erupted in Europe, Switzerland's mercenary contracts were either finished, or if they were not finished, they were instead neutralized by being in service to parties on opposite sides of the conflict. Even while the cantons were in religious conflict, they agreed overall about removing Swiss soldiers from foreign military involvement. Only the Swiss Papal Guard remained in effect.

Historically, the Thirty Years' War was thought to be a German civil war combined with aspects of the Reformation; more recently historians have linked the underlying cause to rivalry between the Habsburgs and the French Bourbons. Even now the points are debated right down to the accuracy of the name of the war.

To our viewpoint, however, the importance is that the Swiss Confederacy refused to participate. Borders and alpine passes were closed to foreign armies, and the Confederacy refused alliances with any of the involved monarchs.

There was only one exception to this strict neutrality, which was to allow the French army to cross the Protestant cantons to the Grisons, which was a sort of federation of loose communes with no centralized government. Though geographically neighbors to Uri and Ticino, the Grisons was not yet a Swiss canton and would not be until 1803. In the chaos of the Thirty Years' War, the Grisons suffered twenty years of war fought on its grounds.

The Peace of Westphalia treaties brought peace to the Holy Roman Empire and concluded the Thirty Years' War. At this convergence, Switzerland emerged as an independent nation recognized by all parties.

The Renaissance in Switzerland

Switzerland, poised directly between Germany and Italy, was swept up in the Renaissance but unlike those countries, did not have the financial capabilities to produce any large, noteworthy structures. Switzerland's contributions to the Renaissance were mostly those of artists, writers, doctors and thinkers. Switzerland's relative open-mindedness also made it a haven for those whose ideas were unwelcome in their home countries.

The city of Basel (canton of Basel-Stadt) became a center of intellectual freedom and learning during the Renaissance. Its university, founded in 1460, is the oldest in Switzerland and was an advocate of humanism, and therefore served as a safe place for notable political refugees driven from, or running from, their own homelands. This would not be the last time that Switzerland opened its borders to those fleeing oppression, as we will see.

Protestant and Huguenot refugees found sanctuary not only in Basel, but in Geneva and Neuchâtel, and a number of these refugees became important contributors to the Swiss watch industry and the iconic Swiss banking industry.

Important Swiss figures during the Renaissance included:

> » Paracelsus, a physician, theologian and alchemist, who taught at the University of Basel. Credited as the "father of toxicology," Paracelsus pioneered many aspects of the Renaissance's medical revolution, including, but certainly not limited to, the use of chemicals and minerals in medicine (such as iron to treat anemia), introduced the ideas of keeping wounds clean and the concept of antisepsis, and was among the first to propose the idea that diseases were entities unto themselves (i.e., germs).

> » Hans Holbein the Younger, a high renaissance painter and renowned portraitist who had great influence on Swiss artists, also spent considerable time teaching in Basel.

> » Conrad Gessner of Zurich served as the City Physician, but it was his studies in linguistics, zoology and botany that made this true Renaissance man famous; he is considered the father of modern scientific bibliography (in fact he wrote a massive universal biography of, in theory, every book ever written), botany and zoology (his *Historiea animalum* was another huge accomplishment; it

was also he who developed the concept of an animal species), and another book accounting about 130 known languages.

» Matthäus Merian of Zurich, who operated a publishing house, produced maps that displayed early scientific cartography. He drew many city plans, published maps of countries and a world in a huge 21-volume set called the *Topographia Germaniae*.

» A number of notable historians emerged at this time:

  » Aegidius Tschudi wrote a history of the early Swiss Confederacy, which gave rise to the tale of William Tell and the valiant oaths taken by the early Swiss canton leaders. He was enormously influential though, after the 19th Century, many of his claims for historical resources were proven to exaggerated or even false, so his histories are to be taken with reservations.

  » Konrad Justinger, Diebold Schilling the Elder, and Diebold Schilling the Younger were some of many notable artists and authors of Swiss illustrated chronicles, were where beautifully illuminated manuscripts produced for the aristocracy that detailed the politics and life of Switzerland prior to the reformation.

  » Valerius Anshelm, a Reformation sympathizer, wrote his Swiss chronicles from the city of Bern. His works included a history of Bern, of Switzerland, and a Latin chronicle of world history.

Important printing centers formed in Basel and Geneva; their voluminous output greatly aided the dissemination of ideas. The first newspapers were generated here, though they were short-lived (censored and shut down by the nobility). The cities to Gall, Glarus and Bern also encouraged scholarship and education.

The Helvetic Republic

It seemed that Switzerland was minding its own business, creating cheeses, refining the watchmaking industry and basically getting along fine, when suddenly the Revolutionary French government invaded Switzerland in 1798 – sort of – conquered the country and established a new regime. Two Swiss cantons were allocated to France and to the Cisalpine Republic; the remaining cantons were abolished, the territories united under a constitution. It was the first time that the cantons were under a centralized government, which was called the Helvetic Republic. To the mind of the French revolutionaries, they were "freeing" the Swiss people from an outdated feudal system.

The invasion took place almost bloodlessly, with the French simply stepping in and seizing control, and most of the population unaware, or unwilling to believe, that such a thing could be happening. For some time, a debate had stewed among Swiss leadership. They could not agree on whether Switzerland should become a united republic or an aristocratic regime. Those who wished for a united republic were not averse to the intervention of the French revolutionaries.

This was not a common feeling, however. Finding themselves overtaken and turned into little more than a strategically placed French satellite state, the Swiss reaction was of serious opposition. For centuries they had controlled their destiny, and the people were outraged by this invasion and the destruction of their traditions. The progressiveness of the revolutionary ideas, such as this sudden "freedom of religion" was more shocking to them than welcome.

The Swiss struck back repeatedly at their invaders, attempting coups and inciting skirmishes throughout the land. The Nidwalden Revolt in September 1798 was particularly horrific, when the uprising was quelled by the French burning towns and villages in the canton, seriously damaging the infrastructure and killing around 400 Swiss. Then, when Russian and Austrian forces attacked the French (by invading Switzerland), the Swiss refused to fight for the new Helvetic Republic.

In 1803, Napoleon moved to appease the Swiss, calling a meeting of leading Swiss politicians. As a result, the Act of Mediation was established, restoring Swiss autonomy and reestablishing a confederation made up of 19 cantons.

SWITZERLAND AS A FEDERAL STATE

In 1815, following the Napoleonic wars, the Congress of Vienna re-established Swiss independence and recognized Swiss neutrality. As a neutral territory, Switzerland formed a useful barrier between Italy and Austria – and it is worth mentioning that no one particularly wanted to scrap with the Swiss, who maintained a reputation as frightening, tenacious enemies. Three more cantons joined Switzerland at that time, but since 1815 the borders have remained unchanged save for small adjustments. Power was restored to Swiss nobility.

Despite Swiss disagreement with the Helvetican system of government, the more democratic society it had presented managed to change some Swiss minds about nobility. The Swiss people were no longer happy to follow the rules of the aristocracy. Civil war erupted and some Catholic cantons attempted to set up a separate alliance. The civil war in Switzerland was minor compared to that of other European nations, lasting less than a month and producing less than 100 casualties. Nevertheless, it deeply impacted a society that had long held a strong nationalistic pride. Switzerland's cantons recognized that they could not take the path of their European neighbors; they must unite and strengthen their country, which meant including all political, religious and social groups.

Thus, in 1848, the Swiss produced a federal constitution that borrowed heavily from the American constitution, forming a centralized government though leaving self-government of local issues to the cantons. Two houses formed the national assembly, the "upper" the Council of States (two representatives from each canton) and the "lower" the National Council (representatives elected from throughout the country).

The constitution ended nobility in Switzerland. Switzerland also determined that troops would no longer be sent abroad to serve other governments with two exceptions: the Papal Swiss Guard, and a contract with Francis II, which obligated them to serve him through 1860.

The constitution provided that it could be rewritten completely, should such action become necessary. That provision has been utilized more than once. The Swiss constitution was rewritten in 1874, when a surging population and the Industrial Revolution made several modifications necessary. It was also heavily revised in 1891 to include elements of direct democracy, Switzerland's unusual type of democratic government.

UNDER THE ALPS: THE GOTTHARD TUNNEL

As we have seen, the Gotthard Pass was the preferred method of foot, horse and wagon travel *over* the Alps leading from Switzerland to Italy. In the late 19th Century, Europe recognized the need for a connecting railway between the North Sea and the Mediterranean. So, when technology was ready and the money was available, and it came time to tunnel *under* the Alps, Gotthard was once again chosen for its central point in the mountains. The cost of building the tunnel was divided among Switzerland, Italy, and Germany.

The Gotthard Railway Company (established 1871) was operated by Alfred Escher, a successful Swiss industrialist. After winning the bid, Swiss engineer Louis Favre was hired as the contractor. Surveys of the mountains showed the optimum route between Göschenen and Airolo, but the very layout of the Alps found ordinary surveying techniques and cartography insufficient to correctly lay out the tunnel's projected path; complex geometric calculations were made and then double-checked by separate teams.

Boring began from opposite sides of the tunnel in 1871, with hopeful plans of meeting at the mid-point, the tunnel took ten years to complete. The construction required the use of dynamite, which had only been patented a few years earlier, on a large scale. Favre also used mechanized tunneling machines despite pressures to use manual labor.

Difficulties were expected and came as no surprise. Of the multiple problems that the tunnel construction suffered were the constant need for water (to cool the rock and machines) and compressed air (needed to supply energy to the machinery that transported the water). Huge pipelines were laid along the inside of the tunnel's path to accommodate these needs. Well over 200 workers were killed during construction, from rockslides, water inrushes, explosions, toxic fumes, and mechanical accidents, and also during an unfortunate attempt to strike that was violently put down by the Altdorf police force. At one point, the workers were stricken by an epidemic hookworm infection. While treatment of their infection led to significant advances in parasitology, the workers likely would rather have been parasite-free than contribute to such medical heroism.

Favre, who is credited with the tunnel's impressive engineering, unfortunately died of a heart attack in 1879, only six months before the tunnel's breakthrough – he was within the tunnel at the time of his death. In 1880, the tunnel's two opposite borings connected with impressive accuracy; the innovate and careful surveying had paid off.

The tunnel opened for traffic on January 1, 1882 and was lauded as a monumental achievement. Swiss president Bavier declared, "The Swiss Alps have been breached." The private rail company Gotthardbahn operated the tunnel for a time using steam locomotives, but in 1909 the enterprise was absorbed into Swiss Federal Railways. In 1920, electric trains began to run through the Gotthard Tunnel and by the following year, all steam trains were replaced by electric ones. This significantly improved the pollution conditions inside the tunnel.

The 20th Century saw improvements in engineering to the extent that the Gotthard Tunnel became outdated. In 1980, the Gotthard Road tunnel opened and is now the path of about a million freight trucks every year. (An interesting side note: prior to the development of the road, Swiss Federal Railways offered "piggyback" services for vehicles, allowing cars and trucks to sit on the trains that passed through the tunnel.) The Gotthard Base Tunnel, another railway, opened in 2016. The Base Tunnel, 17 years in construction, is over 50 km longer than the original Gotthard Tunnel (making it the longest tunnel in the world) but because it runs a straight route at higher speeds, it is more energy and time efficient.

WORLD WAR I

During the first World War, Switzerland was bordered on every side by warring nations. Germany and Austria-Hungary, Central Powers, vied against France and Italy, Entente Powers. Caught in between, Switzerland's neutrality was difficult to maintain. Germany had plans to violate Swiss neutrality and march straight through to outflank France's fortifications; it was only due to the mountainous terrain of Switzerland that Belgium, which reputedly also had less well-organized defenses, was selected to serve as the passageway to France.

Far from helpless, the Swiss Army at the time consisted of almost a quarter million troops with a nearly equal-sized support network. Early in the war, Swiss troops were stationed all along the Jura range and in the Unterengadin regions to keep France and Italy's trench wars from spilling over into Swiss territory. There were some violent encounters in these areas, with gunfire exchanged when foreign troops crossed the border.

Naturally, because Switzerland was largely divided between German, French and Italian-speaking citizens, there were internal conflicts and sides chosen, and Allied blockades caused economic difficulties. But despite these problems, Switzerland still managed to stay out of the war. When it became clear that its neutrality would be respected by all sides, many of the Swiss troops were allowed to return to their homes. They regathered when once more it seemed a foreign army would cross the country (this time, French forces) but this, too, failed to happen. By the end of World War I, only about 12,500 men remained in service.

While Switzerland remained neutral and mostly undamaged, its banking industry thrived while other European economies crumbled.

The country once again became a haven for political refugees and pacifists, and debate thrived among these modern thinkers about the ethics of war. From Zurich emerged two anti-war groups:

1. **The Dadaists**, inspired by the art movement, centered their protests about the illogical nature of conflict around abstract art, theater, and writings, and after the war they returned to their own countries to further the pacificism movement through artistic influence.

2. **The Bolsheviks** sprang from the Russian Social Democratic Labour Party. Vladimir Lenin came to Switzerland from Austria in 1914 and remained there

until 1917, actively promoting his outraged stance that when Social Democratic Parties supported this war, they were forcing the working class to basically fight for the sake of their class enemies. Lenin returned to Petrograd in 1917 to lead the October Revolution in Russia.

Switzerland opened its mountain resorts to serve as recovery facilities for almost 70,000 British, German, and French troops. The wounded soldiers were transferred from prisoner of war camps; they were either injured to the extent that their military service could not continue, or they had been imprisoned for more than 18 months and were suffering deteriorating mental health. This program was organized by the Red Cross, and the warring parties agreed to the terms.

In 1917, the scandal of the Grimm-Hoffman Affair disrupted the Swiss government and momentarily called the country's neutrality into question. Swiss Federal Councilor Arthur Hoffman sent socialist politician Robert Grimm to Russia to attempt negotiations for a separate peace deal between Germany and Russia. However, Hoffman had not consulted the remaining members of the Swiss government, even as Grimm presented himself as a full representative of the Swiss government. When the Allies discovered that such negotiations were taking place, Grimm was forced to return home and Hoffman had to resign his position.

BETWEEN WORLD WARS

For about twenty years, Switzerland was an island of calm in the devastated European landscape. Even so, several important events occurred in the years between the First and Second World War.

> » Burdened by the failing Germanic economies, Lichtenstein separated itself from Austria's influence. It instead signed agreements with Switzerland to guarantee the survival of its economy – the two little countries would thereafter share a currency and trade rules.

> » Switzerland joined the League of Nations in 1920 but withdrew once more in 1938 when it seemed that war in Europe was inevitable.

> » In 1934, the passing of the Swiss Banking Act allowed for anonymous numbered bank accounts to be established. This was, in part, to allow Germans (including German Jews) to move their money and assets out of the reach of the Third Reich.

» Considering growing European tensions, the Swiss began to prepare once more for war. Councilor Rudolf Minger led the rebuilding of the Swiss Army (with updated training regimens), procured a larger defense budget, and began a program of war bonds. At home, citizens were encouraged to have hold enough supplies for two months. Minger predicted, quite accurately, that war would come in 1939.

» The public propaganda policy of *Geistige Landesverteidigung* was heavily promoted; this was a concerted effort to prove Switzerland's independent national identity. Its primary purpose was to separate Switzerland from the fascist powers that surrounded it.

World War II

Switzerland easily mobilized for a possible invasion at the outbreak of the war in 1939; the country was well-prepared for the contingency. Led by General Henri Guisan, the Swiss military fully mobilized more than half a million troops (including support services) within three days.

The neutral status of Switzerland during the Second World War was maintained by luck, the deterrence of their considerable military force, and concessions to Germany that delayed and/or prevented invasion. Because Swiss trade was blockaded by both Axis and Allied powers, cooperation with the Third Reich occurred in the form of trade and extended credit, though the rate of cooperation depended on extenuating circumstances: first, whether other trading opportunities were available; and second, the likelihood of a German invasion and the need to pacify the Third Reich.

Switzerland, for better or worse, found it safest to remain in a situation where Germany considered them more useful as a trading partner and neutral ground than as another abducted German state.

In 1942, links with the Allied forces were severed by the German possession of France. Concessions to Germany reached their peak at this time. Generally, the Swiss press spoke out firmly against the Nazi Regime, which angered the Swiss government, which was trying to avert German invasion.

During the war, Switzerland served both Axis and Allied powers in several capacities:

1. The country served as a base for espionage from both sides. The United States set up its Office of Strategic Services ("OSS") office in Bern; it was from this location that the invasion of Italy was organized and directed.

2. Often communications between the Axis and Allied powers were mediated by Switzerland.

3. More than 300,000 refugees were interned within Switzerland, although some of the immigration practices came under criticism and scrutiny, particularly at points when Jewish refugees were refused admission. On its surface, this was a problem of definitions: the Swiss would only grant asylum to those persecuted for their actions, but not to those persecuted based on their ethnicity, race, or religion.

Both Axis and Allied powers violated Swiss airspace; Switzerland's Air Force had engagements from both Axis and Allied fighter plans, and many of its cities suffered bombings. Luftwaffe planes that slipped over the borders were either shot or forced down. The Allies actively bombed Swiss cities, resulting in both structural damage and fatalities. The Allies insisted that these bombings were errors, mistaking the Swiss towns for German or Austrian ones, but the Swiss felt that these bombings were deliberate retribution for Switzerland's trade agreements with Axis powers. After one particularly grim "accidental" bombing resulted in 50 dead Swiss citizens and the destruction of several manufacturing plants (which were, perhaps coincidentally, making parts for Germany), Switzerland issued a zero-tolerance policy for any planes invading its airspace. Eventually, English pilots who bombed Swiss towns faced court-martial, and the United States paid hefty reparations for structural damages.

During the war, the Swiss National Bank bought large amounts of gold from both the Allies and the Germans, in exchange for Swiss francs or other foreign currencies that could be used to purchase raw materials from other neutral countries. Millions of francs of this gold were stolen from the banks and citizens of occupied countries, and from victims of the Holocaust.

Toward the end of the 20th Century, the ethics Switzerland's policy of concessions to Germany during World War II came under serious attack. The Swiss government commissioned a study of Switzerland's interaction with the Nazis; the final report was issued in 2002 and is known as the Bergier Commission. One of the results of this report was to admit Switzerland's role in the sale of art looted by the Nazis. Switzerland, however, was not entirely free in its choices of trading partners. The country relied on trade for approximately half of its food and almost all its fuel supplies. Switzerland feared that Germany would withdraw the coal supplies it provided to them, for example, if Switzerland refused to transport the German coal meant for Italy. So, despite Allied pressures, these transactions continued.

Swiss concessions to the Third Reich indeed involved some distasteful bedfellows and, in hindsight, some poor decisions. It is hard to feel sorry for the bullied Swiss while their banks became filthy rich in stolen money. It is known that some Swiss officials were Nazi sympathizers; but naturally, others were not. In all fairness, we must view the actions (or inactions) of Switzerland for what they were: an attempt to stave off invasion, and perhaps to make the best of a frightening situation. In desperate times, actions taken are not always the noblest. Switzerland itself must live with its history, and in many ways, it continues to make amends, with its numerous organizations and contributions to the modern stage of promoting peace and prosperity throughout the world.

The National Redoubt

During World War II, invasion plans for Switzerland were developed by the German Army, such as Operation Tannenbaum. Had it not been for the Allied landing at Normandy and difficulties Germany faced in invading the Soviet Union, Switzerland would have almost certainly been overtaken by Germany and Italy, who planned to divide the country between them.

But invasion, planned or otherwise, might not have been as easy as rolling over the border. Switzerland had rethought its defense strategy. Rather than using a border defense, Switzerland turned its defenses to a plan of attrition and withdrawal to hidden fortresses within the Alps, an idea long in development, that was termed the Swiss National Redoubt.

The Swiss National Redoubt was a plan of considerable expense and controversial strategy: its purpose was to make the cost of invading Switzerland so high that it was not worth the effort. The Swiss Army would, in effect, surrender the visible portion of the country to invaders, but retain control of all that essentially could make the country run: the rail lines, the mountain passes, electricity.

The idea of the Redoubt had been in play since the 1880s, and in fact it used much of the same technology that was used to dig the original Gotthard Tunnel. With a Second World War looming large, the Swiss government expanded and refined the plans, and the jobs created by doubling down on building the redoubt were useful during the worldwide Great Depression.

The Alps were quietly and thoroughly outfitted with an enormous network of caverns that served as a well-defended hiding place, and guarded the vital passes through the mountains, making passage through the Alps impossible. With the country thus immobilized, it should be useless to aggressors. The Alps are honeycombed with military installations, including living quarters for anywhere from 100 to 600 troops, underground dams to produce electricity, hospitals, and airstrips, and supplies sufficient for an indefinite stay underground.

The Redoubt caused considerable controversy within the country, not only in its expense but in the fact that it basically left the heavily populated plateau at the mercy of invading forces while the government and military sought refuge in the Alps. This is probably why the majority of the Swiss people were not informed of the plan until the country was virtually surrounded by Axis powers and in imminent danger of invasion.

THE COLD WAR

Swiss authorities recognized the possibility of entering the nuclear arms race. Switzerland had capable physicists at the Federal Institute of Technology. Defense budget limitations, along with ethical concerns, prevented such plans from going beyond the stage of talks. The Nuclear Non-Proliferation Treaty was a measure promoting the peaceful use of nuclear energy through international cooperation. The treaty was negotiated by the Eighteen Nation Committee on Disarmament, a Geneva organization sponsored by the United Nations. Switzerland, as the birthplace of the treaty, signed on in 1968 once the details of the Treaty were completed. Plans for developing nuclear weapons in Switzerland were ceased, at least formally, by 1988.

While Switzerland may not have developed its own nuclear arsenal, they were not inactive in preparing for possible Cold War outcomes. The National Redoubt, as established in World War II, was updated and adapted for the needs predicted in a nuclear war and the following nuclear winter. Electrical dams, shelters and defensive weapons were kept up to date deep in their Alpine hiding places.

To thwart invaders on the ground, the roads and bridges of the country were rigged with demolitions, which would permit the Swiss to destroy any important routes at a moment's notice. It is estimated that some 3,000 explosive charges were laid on Switzerland's thoroughfares.

Since the end of the Cold War, Switzerland has been decommissioning and gradually dismantling these preparations. They eventually removed the explosives from bridges and roads. Alternative uses have been found for the extensive networks of caverns drilled into the Alps. Many underground facilities have been purchased by companies who use the inherent benefits of Alpine caverns to their advantage; the conditions are perfect for the requirements of massive electronic data storage. Some of the caverns have even been opened as museums.

Still, Switzerland is far from a vulnerable country. The government funded the building of shelters in most Swiss homes, so that a surprising majority of older Swiss houses are equipped with bomb shelters. Among the barns and houses of little mountain towns, it is not unusual to discover a concrete bunker disguised as farm building, with a working air defense gun inside. And of course, Swiss men are required to spend time in the military and the reserves, so that roughly two thirds of Swiss men have military training and most retain guns, ammunition, and gas masks in their homes.

SWITZERLAND AND THE EUROPEAN UNION

The Swiss government has long desired to join the European Union, but the popular sentiment (led by the large conservative party) is against joining, and as a direct democracy, the votes of the people are taken at their value. To offset the potential disadvantages of non-membership, Switzerland has developed numerous relationships with the Union that comply with understandings membership would have achieved, and has also structured its economic practices to match those of the Union. Bern and Brussels have adopted trade agreements to offset the negative effects of separation (these include the free movement of persons throughout Europe, i.e., "passport-free" zones) and many other areas of cooperation with the Union. Among these are investing in poorer Southern/Central European countries, opening their electricity market, participation in project Galileo (the EU's Global Satellite Navigation System), and participation in the European center for disease prevention. Recent Swiss voting has reflected increasing support for these bilateral agreements with the European Union.

THE THINGS SHE'S FAMOUS FOR

Now let's have a look at three export industries for which Switzerland is known worldwide.

THE SWISS CHEESE EMPIRE

Humans have been making cheese for about as long as we've been drinking milk. Cheese-making techniques have developed and been perfected over our entire history. The Romans were especially known for their cheese technology using rennet (animal stomach lining) to craft sturdy cheeses that could be aged. As the Romans spread their culture throughout the world, they also brought their cheese-production techniques to the world's inhabitants.

The first historical record of "Swiss" cheese comes from the 1st Century Roman historian Pliny the Elder: he described "Caseus Helveticus," the cheese of the Helvetians.

Until the early Middle Ages, Switzerland was a self-sufficient country. The Alps were dominated by farms and herds of goats and cattle, and wherever milk was made it had to be preserved. It was turned into products that lasted longer, such as butter, quark and ziger (whey cheese). Much trial, error, and pure hard work over hundreds of years went into the creation of cheeses that could survive the transport time necessary to make cheese a valuable export.

In the early 15th Century, the Catholic Church, with its massive property resources and seemingly endless supply of monks to work menial tasks, took the initiative and put in the time and effort to experiment and see what techniques were most effective in the production of cheese. The Church also loosened fasting laws in the northern Alpine regions so that dairy products could be eaten during Lent and other church holidays. They experimented with different cooking techniques, types of milk, how long milk could be aged and stored. Once they got a hold of rennet, their magnificent cheeses could last much longer, and cheese became a part of European traveler's everyday lives. These monks kept stocks of cheese for guests.

Among the many cheeses invented by monks throughout Europe were Roquefort, muenster, and parmesan. The best-known Swiss cheeses are Alpine cheeses, such as Emmental, Gruyere and Appenzeller. Neighboring Alpine regions all had (and still have) their own varieties. Their distinct character arose from cheese-making requirements and the different grasses on which the cattle fed throughout the summer. These cheeses made were shaped into "wheels" with a hard rennet rind so that they could stay fresh and hold a great shelf-life.

In the Confederation's early days, cheese was considered a principal food. It was even accepted as a form of currency: "Paid in cheese and money." Gruyere cheese was so profitable, its production facilities were raided by envious cheesemakers of neighboring Swiss cantons so the secrets of its cheese production could be discovered. Alpine herdsmen used to carry their wheels of cheese over the Alpine passes to Italy and trade them for spices, wine, chestnuts, and rice. Distinct local differences in cheeses emerged due to different mountain pasture sizes, various methods of production and methods of treatment - for example, cows that spent summertime in mountain pastures could produce larger cheese wheels.

By the 1700s, cheese was Switzerland's most valuable trading commodity, and it was sold everywhere around Europe. According to an actual 1793 travel guide: "Even in the regions which produce a lot of milk, it is hard to get good cream for your coffee or fresh butter, because the locals find it more profitable to make cheese out of their milk." People believed that long-lasting cheese (the sort that could survive travel) could only be produced in the Alps.

Then in 1805, Phillip Emanuel von Fellenberg experimented with his own dairy on his Hofwil estate and proved that good cheese could be made in the lowlands too. Then in 1815, Rudolf Emanuel von Effinger, lord of Kiesen castle, developed Emmental – the cheese with the distinctive holes. The Swiss were skeptical about this so-called "valley" cheese, but the flavor grew very popular and the ease of production was such that by 1832, valley-dairies popped up everywhere.

Emmental cheese's popularity was also boosted because it contained no lactose. The lactose was broken down in the production process. Most of the world is lactose intolerant, thus people loved Emmental. The Swiss cheese holes come from microscopically tiny hay particles that get unintentionally mixed into buckets of milk. These holes expand as the cheese matures. The process for making Emmental was expanded to develop other low and no-lactose cheeses.

For Switzerland, this was the great age of cheese. The canton of Bern alone exported almost 23,000 hundredweights of cheese in 1834. Dairies were so numerous in the Alpine regions that Swiss cheesemakers were forced to leave Switzerland to find markets elsewhere that weren't so crowded and had more room for the necessary agriculture. Swiss cheesemakers became almost as valuable an export as was the cheese itself. The United States welcomed thousands of cheese-making Swiss immigrants.

By 1875, fortunes had been invested in the cheese trade, but supply was beginning to outpace demand. Just as many dairy farmers made cheese quickly, cheaply, and incorrectly as those who made a quality product. In other cases, dairymen sold inferior product to locals while saving their higher-quality cheese for exports. Products like milk and butter, as bemoaned by the tourist pamphlet, were so difficult and expensive to find that the market for cheese fell into ruins. Family businesses were destroyed as "trust" in cheese production failed.

To resolve this cheese catastrophe and regain their reputations, the cheesemakers of Switzerland united in reform. They agreed to decrease the quantity of cheese but increase the quality. Dairy schools were opened to give cheesemakers the opportunity to improve their craft. Cheesemakers were taught the importance of livestock stabling and were given in-depth knowledge of feeding cattle. Cheesemakers had to be certified to sell product on the market.

In 1913, fears over war in Europe made the Swiss concerned about supplies and possible food shortages. The Swiss government wanted sole authority over who could or could not export Swiss cheese, so it created The Association of Swiss Cheese Export Firms. Later, the ASCEF became the Swiss Cheese Union. The Swiss Cheese Union expanded their reach into quality control as well as export rights monitoring.

Over the course of the 20th Century, rigorous standards were introduced into the world of Swiss cheese. The variety of cheeses allowed for production were limited to fourteen types. Of those, even fewer were endorsed for manufacture and export, such as Emmental and Gruyere.

But where money can be made, corruption can flourish. The Swiss Cheese Union became far too big and controlling for its own good. It had arms in Swiss government, bombarded newspapers with cheese advertisements, and even took bribes to provide certain sellers with special treatment and opportunities. In 1999, the World Trade Organization disbanded the Union.

Today, Swiss cheese makers are back on top. Switzerland has more than 475 varieties of cheese. According to industry figures, the people of Switzerland alone ate 186,756 tons of cheese, averaging about 22kg per person per year. The top-produced variety of Swiss cheese is Le Gruyere, of which more than 28,500 tons was produced in 2015. Mozzarella is second, then Emmentaler, séré (the Swiss-French word for fromage frais) and Raclette. The continued production and exportation of cheese supports the strong economic backbone of Switzerland.

The Fine Chocolatiers

Until the Industrial Revolution, chocolate was predominantly available in the form of a drink, and accessible only to the wealthy.

By 1806, the Swiss town of Vevey was busy with factories: some for tobacco; some for milk production; and seven small factories open for chocolate production. The chocolate of the time was practically unrecognizable compared to the substance we know today. It was bitter, grainy, gritty, and unpleasant. These unsweetened chunks of cacao were liquefied into hot beverages, and often prescribed by druggists as tonics and elixirs, at a very high cost. The wealthy indulged in chocolate, believing it to be a symbol of status and that consuming it improved one's energy and well-being.

After developing a taste for chocolate at Italian fairs, enthusiast François-Louis Cailler lived in Italy for four years to learn the crafting of chocolate. He then set up his own factory near Vevey in 1819, feeling that the product's potential was untapped. He invented a machine-pressed chocolate that allowed for mass-production. He tried to establish a chocolate-selling business model, and in doing so learned that making chocolate had a lot of setbacks. Cocoa beans had to be imported from South America. He never knew how many beans he could get or when they would arrive, and they were quite costly, as were sugar and the production processes. Solid chocolate was bitter and crumbly so Cailler continued producing chocolate in liquid form to sell to wealthy customers. Still, Cailler became the first recognizable chocolate entrepreneur of his kind, paving the way for other chocolate innovators.

In the canton of Neuchâtel in 1826, Phillippe Suchard opened a two-man factory named Chocolat Suchard. His factory utilized a nearby river to generate hydropower for his mills. He invented a mixing machine for cocoa that added fair amounts of sugar. Then, his grinding mills used heated granite plates and granite rollers to grind cocoa paste. Suchard's commercial process made chocolate far tastier, but the substance still lacked an acceptable texture, it was undesirably crumbly and gritty. Cocoa paste was also pricey to produce. Nevertheless, a huge order for chocolate from the King of Prussia bolstered Suchard's struggling business and brought attention to the product throughout Europe.

Swiss businessman Charles-Amadeé Kohler established his own factory in Lausanne, 1830. Kohler had the idea to mix hazelnuts into chocolate (hazelnuts even in the modern era continue to be Switzerland's most popular chocolate mix-in). Hazelnuts improved chocolate's flavor-profile, yet the form of chocolate remained unmanageable.

Let's turn back to the Cailler factory near Vevey. By 1867 Cailler's daughter was married to Vevey candlemaker Daniel Peter. The increasing popularity of oil lamps was damaging the candle business, so Peter and his brother-in-law, Cailler's son, bought the chocolate factory. Peter too saw potential in chocolate but knew that the substance needed further improvement, and hopefully, a way for their product to distinguish itself among competition. Peter searched for any opportunity to improve his own product. A neighbor also interested in food production provided some valuable input to the process; his name was Henri Nestlé.

Nestlé wanted to make his own baby-food formula and thus experimented with powdered milks produced from the abundant population of Alpine cows. Powdered milk was a step in the right direction, improving the flavor of chocolate immensely, but the mixture required a high water content that caused substance separation and was susceptible to mildew. The inventors decided to substitute condensed milk for powdered.

For seven years of trial and error, chocolate hopefuls Peter and Nestlé continued their work in Vevey and figured out just the right mixture of chocolate and condensed milk until they eventually invented milk chocolate with a creamy, smooth character.

Their milk-chocolate was so successful that Daniel Peter and Henri Nestlé created the Nestlé Company in 1879.

That same year, Swiss manufacturer Rudolf Lindt invented conching machines. These conching machines were the final piece of the puzzle that led to truly great chocolate with the delightful property of melting in the mouth. In terms of chocolate, texture is every bit as important as taste. Conching is a technique used on milk, in which its fat content is emulsified, and the cream doesn't separate. It involves intense mixing and aeration of hot liquid chocolate, sifting through its contents and eliminating unwanted bitterness and acidity. It is roughly the equivalent process of milk homogenization and pasteurization.

Lindt's conching machine design was sold to other chocolatiers in the 1890s, and such machines were soon utilized by The Nestlé Company and then by any other chocolate entrepreneur who wanted to stay in business. The Nestlé Company created the first real bar of milk chocolate, often called "Peter" bars. It was solid and sturdy could be bitten through it and the chocolate would "melt in your mouth." The Nestlé Company made sure that bars of chocolate were inexpensive, turning chocolate from a privilege for the wealthy into an enormously popular affordable treat, with marketing directed toward women and children. Today, The Nestlé Company still has Daniel Peter's original milk-chocolate recipe book.

Between the 19th and early 20th Century is when the popularity of Swiss chocolate spread beyond its borders and marked Switzerland's ascension to chocolate royalty. Chocolate advertisements deliberately emphasized the fact that good chocolate comes from Switzerland. Advertisements shows the Alps and their cows that produce great Alpine milk.

Even beyond Lindt and Nestlé, Switzerland is home to many small award-winning chocolate houses. While less widely known outside Switzerland, they produce some of the finest chocolate in the world. Chocolate has been one of the country's top exports since the 1900s.

A Question of Time: Swiss Clocks and Watches

Clock and watchmaking did not originate in Switzerland. France and Germany, separately, were the countries that innovated timepieces first. The first geared clocks were created around the start of the 14th Century. These pieces were large and therefore stationary. In the mid-1600s the first pendulum clock was developed and is still used today in some instances such as in traditional grandfather clocks. Germany developed a miniaturized clock small enough to be worn and to qualify as a "watch," somewhere between 1509 and 1530, an item affordable only by the extremely wealthy. Despite a commonly quoted line from *The Third Man* (1949) that playfully mocks Swiss neutrality, the Swiss did not invent the cuckoo clock; cuckoo clocks were originally a product of the Black Forest area in Germany.

The Reformation saw the intense persecution of protestants, such as the Huguenots of France, who fled to Geneva, bringing their watchmaking skills along with them. Coincidentally, John Calvin was leading the Reformation in Geneva and declared that wearing jewelry was a sin of pride and was thus forbidden. The numerous jewelers, goldsmiths and enamellers of Geneva scrambled to find a way to make up for the loss of income and cleverly realized that watches could be considered necessary tools rather than jewelry. They threw in their efforts into watchmaking. With the technical knowledge of the Huguenots and the craftsmanship of Geneva's jewelry artisans, watches of significant quality were created.

With this influx of skilled workers, and the booming demand for watches, Geneva soon became known for its timepieces. The industry was so prosperous that the area became glutted with watch manufacturers, causing many such businesses to seek new territories for their factories in the Jura mountains.

In the 18th Century, Britain dominated the pocket watch industry, a consumer demand that emerged with the popularity of waistcoats. To accommodate growing needs for improved tech, inventions including the tooth cutting machine, the balance spring, chronometers, and lever escapement improved the accuracy of timepieces. Switzerland contributed innovations as well, including the "perpetual" watch (created by Abraham-Louis Perrelet), a predecessor of the self-winding watch. The pendant winding watch was developed by Adrien Phillipe, one of the founders of Patek Philippe. Swiss-born inventor Abraham-Louis Breguet in 1801 invented the tourbillon, an exquisite watchmaking device that counters the effect of gravity drag on timepieces. Even in the modern era, a tourbillon is an expensive addition to a watch. French watchmaker Jean-Antoine Lépine invented his namesake calibre, notably thinner than previous models, which allowed the development of smaller and thinner pocket watches.

The Swiss were quick to incorporate advantageous designs into their timepiece production. But it was the flexibility and the decentralization of Switzerland that gave its biggest advantage in the world of time. The Swiss streamlined watch production. Early innovation is credited to goldsmith Daniel Jeanrichard (of the Neuchâtel canton), who applied the division of labor to watchmaking, increasing both efficiency of productions and standardization of the products. By 1790, Geneva was exporting approximately 60,000 watches each year.

This process was called *établissage*, but in simple terms it is the assembly-line production of watches, with the caveat that parts may be made elsewhere and then delivered to the line for inspection and then incorporation into the assembly. For example, to supplement their income in the winter, Swiss farmers worked making watch components for the firms in Geneva. Their flexibility combined with their streamlined work process (which the French and British refused to adopt) meant that Switzerland could mass-produce watches and jump ahead of its competition.

To illustrate the point, in 1800, both Switzerland and Britain produced about 200,000 timepieces. By 1850, however, Britain continued to produce slightly more than 200,000, whereas Switzerland produced well over two million.

The only drawback was that, in mass-production of timepieces, the Swiss manufacturers were not focusing as intensely on quality. The American production of watches rose just as the French and British markets fell, and American timepieces were of noticeably higher quality than the mass-produced Swiss watches. Though there were still some Swiss watch companies who were making high-quality pieces, the market was flooded with cheap, lower-quality Swiss watches.

In 1868, American Florentine A. Jones moved to Switzerland to open the International Watch Company. He brought with him the American optimized production process, keeping it all in-house, which ensured the reliability of the watches over those produced by établissage. Many Swiss companies (Longines, for one) quickly saw the advantages and followed suit, combining the qualities of optimized production with the beauty and craftsmanship of traditional Swiss timepieces. As a result, production remained high but the quality of the product improved.

The next wave of inventions in watchmaking were machines (by Pierre-Frédéric Ingold and Georges-Auguste Léschot) that could produce identical and interchangeable watch parts, another huge leap forward in watch tech, as watches could now be more easily repaired, and parts were almost a guaranteed fit.

Wristwatches have an interesting history. The small portable German timepieces of centuries before were precursors of the idea, but actual wristwatches were introduced in World War I, as pocket watches could not be effectively carried by soldiers. Inventive soldiers began tying their watches to their wrists with leather straps. Watches that could fasten to wrists were soon produced; for a brief time, they were called "trench watches" and some even had protective casings to stop shrapnel damage. Genuine trench watches are highly valuable collectors' items.

Today, watches are Switzerland's third-largest export, or 1.5% of the gross domestic product. Watch manufacturing employs almost 60,000 people. Switzerland is home to about 700 watch manufacturers, most of them located in Geneva and the Jura Arc. The market has fluctuated over the years, as one might expect, with technological advances and competition from other nations (such as the rise of Japanese quartz technology, which was countered by an aggressive marketing campaign of the Swatch brand, and, currently, the popularity of Apple watches). Switzerland invented the first wristwatch, the first water-resistant watch, the thinnest and smallest wristwatches, the first quartz watch in 1967, and the world's most expensive watch, then LED and LCD displays, new watchmaking materials, and watches that require no batteries.

In 1971, to protect the integrity of its watch exports, Switzerland defined the legal standards by which a watch brand could be labeled as "Swiss." These standards met with some disagreement among Swiss watchmakers and therefore were revised in 1995.

- » The regulations first define the difference between a watch and a clock (the difference is in their dimensions of movement)
- » The regulations then define circumstances under which those dimensions of movement may be considered Swiss, which include that:
  - » The movement is Swiss
  - » 60 percent of the watch's value is accounted for by Swiss components
  - » The movement was cased in Switzerland
  - » The manufacturer's final inspection takes place in Switzerland
- » Foreign-made watches that use Swiss parts can claim to contain Swiss movement but cannot be called Swiss watches.

Watches made prior to 1971 were not required to meet these standards, and therefore may either fail to meet the qualifications of a Swiss watch or, alternately, may far exceed the requirements.

Modern Switzerland

What is Direct Democracy?

Whereas most western countries practice representative democracies, Switzerland's political system uses components of direct democracy at all government levels. In a direct democracy, every citizen's vote counts. Citizens can propose constitutional changes through popular initiative or ask for operational referendums to be held on laws. A certain number of supporting signatures must be obtained from other Swiss citizens (or 50,000 signatures for referendums; 100,000 for amendments) and then the issue will be put to the vote.

This system of voting puts more power in the hands of individual citizens, but also involves quite regular voting requirements. For example, Swiss citizens have voted 31 times on 103 federal questions and many more questions at the cantonal and municipal levels, between 1995 and 2005. Citizens are called vote on any type of issue at any political level. Simple majority vote is enough to win elections at municipal and cantonal levels; federal/constitutional level requires double majority votes to pass, meaning that a majority of individuals *plus* a majority of cantons' votes are required. Therefore, a constitutional amendment cannot be passed by a majority of personal votes in favor, if a majority of the cantons do not also agree.

In many ways direct democracy is an enviable system that puts the decision-making directly into the hands of a country's people, particularly in view of the relative ease of subversion and corruption in a representative system. However, it is important to distinguish that Switzerland's relatively small population makes direct democracy possible; one-to-one voting increases in difficulty and expense proportionately to increases in population numbers. Switzerland also has tough citizenship requirements, which reduce the number of available voters. Increasing technological capabilities may make direct democracy a more feasible possibility in the future for larger countries desiring to make a change.

On this subject, Switzerland was the last of the Western republics to grant the right to vote to women, and the right was granted piecemeal, first by some (but not all) cantons in 1959, at the federal level in 1971, and then finally the last holdout cantons in 1990. Once they achieved the federal level of suffrage, women rose quickly in Swiss politics. Switzerland's first female president was Ruth Dreifuss, elected in 1999.

In the modern era, Switzerland's executive power is shared by a committee of seven with a rotating, ceremonial president. The committee is strongly in favor of finding consensus.

Citizenship in Switzerland

Because of Switzerland's low crime rate (one of the lowest in the world, in fact), wealth, progressive nature, healthy environment, politics and neutrality, Swiss citizenship is highly sought-after and therefore, not easy to obtain. But in the past twenty years, citizenship laws have undergone some dramatic changes.

There are three paths to becoming Swiss:

1. **Birth**. However, a child is not granted citizenship merely for being born on Swiss soil. A child is granted Swiss citizenship only if:
   a. his/her married parents include at least one Swiss citizen
   b. his/her unmarried mother is Swiss.
   c. his/her unmarried Swiss father acknowledges paternity before the child turns legal age.

2. **Marriage to a Swiss citizen**. Note, this is not automatic. If one marries a Swiss citizen, one can "fast-track" naturalization. The spouse *must* be a Swiss citizen at the time of the marriage for these rules to apply. Foreign spouses of Swiss citizens must have lived in Switzerland for a total of five years to apply for fast-track naturalization.

3. **Naturalization**. If one has no blood ties to Switzerland through birth or marriage, one must live in Switzerland for at least ten years (or six childhood years).

d. Knowledge of a national language is required.

e. A residential permit is required.

f. Criminal offenders or people on welfare are theoretically excluded.

g. If these conditions are met, an applicant's request is "green-lighted"; however, at this point the canton in question begins its approval process, and the rules of obtaining citizenship differ from canton to canton.

h. Applicants are expected to be well-integrated into Swiss society, law-abiding, and no danger to Swiss national security.

Swiss people are permitted to hold multiple nationalities, though this rule is restricted to select countries. Switzerland also permits renaturalization to those who lost their citizenship through legal forfeiture. The ease of obtaining a Swiss citizenship increases dramatically if one can prove descent from Swiss parents or grandparents.

SWITZERLAND AS A WORLD CENTER

Switzerland has diplomatic relations with most countries. Because of its neutrality, it has been able to serve as an impartial intermediary between nations. This, along with the relative ease of doing business within the country, has led to Switzerland being an unparalleled gathering place for world organizations.

Not only a huge number of world organizations, but also many large corporations headquarter in Switzerland. Corporations that elect to use Switzerland as their home base must have at least one Swiss citizen on the board of directors.

Among the world organizations that make their home headquarters and/or hold their annual forums in Switzerland are:

1. The Red Cross and the Red Crescent, aid organizations that are independent of each other but operate under the same seven principles: humanity, impartiality, neutrality, independence, voluntary service, unity, and universality. (Geneva)
2. The World Trade Organization (WTO) (Geneva)
3. The International Federation of Association Football (FIFA) (Zurich)
4. The International Ice Hockey Federation (IIHF) (Zurich)
5. The International Olympic Committee (IOC) as well as the Olympic Museum and the Court of Arbitration for Sport (Lausanne)
6. CERN, the world's largest laboratory (Geneva). The facility is dedicated to particle physics research.
7. The Paul Scherrer Institute (canton of Aargau). This important research facility has developed amazing

technologies from Velcro to the scanning tunneling microscope, a Nobel prize-winning creation.

8. The International Telecommunication Union (ITU) (Geneva)

9. The World Health Organization (WHO) (Geneva)

10. The League of Nations (Geneva)

11. The European headquarters of the United Nations (the Palais des Nations – although Switzerland did not join the United Nations until 2002); the country is also host to the United Nations Human Rights Counsel, and the United Nations High Commissioner for Refugees (Geneva)

12. The International Labor Organization (ILO) (Geneva)

13. The World Economic Forum holds its annual meetings (Davos)

14. Bank for International Settlements (BIS) (Basel)

SWISS MILITARY TODAY

Switzerland, being landlocked, has no navy, but as it also shares lakes with the borders of other countries, it does employ armed military boat patrols. Due to the country's neutrality, the Swiss military does not serve in wars, but they are often called upon for aid and peacekeeping missions. Its Land Forces and Air Force are composed of conscripts: men typically are conscripted at the age of 18 and about two-thirds of them are found fit for service. If they are not suited to service, alternate service exists. Women are permitted to volunteer for service. In 2003, the size of the Swiss army was reduced by popular vote to about 200,000 troops, with 120,000 of those on active duty and 80,000 in reserves. Soldiers keep their military equipment, including all their weapons, and so many a Swiss closet would yield some surprising contents. 29% of Swiss citizens are legal gun owners and the majority of these are guns issued by the Swiss army. However, the army no longer issues ammunition. The Swiss engage in a great deal of recreational shooting and many children belong to gun clubs.

Twice, a referendum has been proposed to eliminate the Swiss military altogether, but both times it has failed by fairly overwhelming majority vote. The second such vote was held just after the September 11, 2001 terrorist attacks on the United States, which probably explains a great deal of the resistance against eliminating military power.

THE SWISS ECONOMY

One of the world's strongest and most stable economies, Switzerland is ranked as the world's wealthiest country per capita across several ranking systems. The country is lauded for its "ease of doing business," global competitiveness and innovation. Strangely, while Switzerland itself is referred to as largely free of corruption, its banking system is criticized, even by the Swiss people themselves, as almost irredeemably corrupt.

Home to several huge multinational corporations, Switzerland's most important economic sector lies in manufacturing. Its most produced products are health products and pharmaceuticals, precise scientific instruments, chemicals, and musical instruments, while its leading exports are chemicals, electronics and machines, and precision instruments (including watches). Next, Switzerland's service industry holds an important economic position, promoting banking, its international organizations, insurance, and tourism.

Taxation is relatively low, however, though comparisons of the tax rates do not include the budgets of cantons and municipalities. Nevertheless, the Swiss federal government's main source of funding comes more from the value-added tax than from direct federal tax.

Just more than 5 million people in Switzerland are employed; they have a highly flexible job market and very low unemployment rates; it was measured at merely 2.3% in 2019 after hovering around 3% for several years prior to that. Switzerland's population has approximately 8.2% living below the poverty line, and another 4.3% qualify as the working poor, meaning that their jobs are low-paying (roughly one in every ten Swiss jobs qualifies as such). Foreigners make up about 25% of the population of Switzerland. Of the available employment in the country, women and foreigners are the most likely to hold jobs that are considered to pay at the "poverty" level.

Mysteries of the Swiss Bank Account

The legendary "Swiss Bank Account" carries iconic status in the popular culture. What is means, simply, is that whether you have ten dollars or ten million dollars in a Swiss bank account, no one (including your nation's tax authorities or your ex-spouse) can access the information. Your balance, your deposits, your withdrawals, everything simple and complex about your bank account, is kept secret. The accounts are numbered, not named.

Switzerland's powerful banking complex actually developed through its merchant trade role in the 18th Century, and even then, client confidentiality was of importance. The Swiss practiced banking secrecy to protect, and draw, the interests of wealthy Europeans. Disclosure of their assets was forbidden, which can of course protect one from any number of pesky taxes, tithes, or expectations. Prominently, Catholic French Kings putting their holdings into Geneva accounts, so that they were not subject to Protestant banks. Then, in the 1780s, Swiss bank accounts began the practice of insuring deposits, which increased their banks' reputation for financial security. Confidentiality of bank customers was held in much the same way as the secrets of the confessional, and even today, disclosing client information is considered a criminal offense.

In 1934, banking secrecy was codified. The Federal Act of Banks and Savings Banks was passed to protect the assets of those persons persecuted by the Nazis; however, this secrecy goes both ways. Not merely the persecuted but the persecutors – and anyone else looking to avoid divulging how much money they have – can take advantage of the system. Financial crime and tax evasion are common and obvious uses for these mysterious secret accounts. Swiss bank accounts are havens for arms dealers, dictators, mobsters, corrupt officials, and tax evaders.

Numerous times, there have been international efforts to seek regulations in Swiss banking and to repeal or lessen secrecy laws; investigations try to probe legal ramifications such as how much the secrecy laws contribute to money laundering. Switzerland's political forces, however, minimize and resist any such efforts. Of course, any "opening" of the information on these massive bank accounts would ruin Switzerland's most profitable business. Despite claims of disapproval from citizens and the world, banking remains dominant in the Swiss economy.

Estimates from the Swiss Bankers Association (SBA) in 2018 put Swiss bank holdings at about $6.5 trillion U.S. Dollars (which equals approximately 25% of all global cross-border assets).

SPEAKING IN SWITZERLAND

There are four national languages in Switzerland:

Language	Location Spoken	Percentage of Population
German*	Mainland, Eastern	62.8
French	Western	22.9
Italian	South	8.2
Romansch	Canton of Grisons	.5

*German is spoken in two dialects: Swiss German (more informal) and Standard German (formal, for business uses).

Nearly two-thirds of the Swiss population speaks more than one language. The government issues documents, communications, and translations into German, Italian and French but Romansch translation of official documents is not required, despite Romansch being an official language.

An interesting linguistic phenomenon occurs here. German and French spoken in Switzerland have developed to contain peculiarities called Helvetisms. These words, which did not come from native German or French, are formed in the melting pot of combined Swiss cultures and the mixing of languages, such as some Italian slipping into German. Modern French and German dictionaries include Helvetisms as part of their languages' vocabularies.

Bilingualism is strongly encouraged. Swiss school pupils are required to learn at least one of the other languages of Switzerland.

EDUCATION AND SCIENCES

Pre-college education is controlled by the cantons, therefore across Switzerland, in both public and private schools, the age requirements for school children, the cost and quality of the schools, and the language curriculums are varied. Once they have completed elementary school, students are typically divided into groups depending on their learning capacities: students who are gifted are put into advanced classes; those who need more dedicated learning are given educations adapted to their needs.

Higher learning is serious business in Switzerland. The twelve universities in Switzerland, many of them ranked among the world's top schools, are also controlled at the canton level. While Basel is the home of the oldest university in Switzerland, Geneva is home to the world's oldest graduate school, the Institute of International and Development Studies. There are two federally funded institutes and many applied science universities.

Some of the world's most famous scientists are affiliated with Switzerland (meaning they were born in Switzerland, or studied and worked in Switzerland); among them:

» Werner Arber, Nobel Prize Medicine, 1978; for discovery of restriction enzymes and their application to molecular genetics

» Felix Bloch, Nobel Prize Physics, 1952; for nuclear magnetic precision measures

» Daniel Bernoulli, the mathematician who found the dynamical equation of fluids

» Albert Einstein, Nobel Prize Physics, 1921; for his groundbreaking contributions to the field of physics

» Charles Guillaume, Nobel Prize Physics, 1920; recognized for his work in precision measurements

» Walter Rudolf Hess, Nobel Prize Medicine, 1949; for mapping of diencephalic function in the brain

» Carl Jung, the founder of analytic psychology, whose work influenced not just the study of psychology but of literature and religion.

» Emil Theodor Kocher, Nobel Prize Medicine, 1909; for his work in physiology and pathology of the thyroid gland

» K. Alex Muller, Nobel Prize Physics, 1987; for discovery of superconductivity studies

» Paul Herman Muller, Nobel Prize Medicine, 1948; for discovery of DDT as a contact poison

» Jean Piaget, a founder and major figure in child psychology

» Tadeus Reichstein, Nobel Prize Medicine, 1950; for work with hormones in the adrenal cortex

» Heinrich Rohrer, Nobel Prize Physics, 1986; for invention of the scanning tunneling microscope (uses particularly in nanotech)

ENERGY AND THE ENVIRONMENT

Switzerland uses 56% hydroelectricity and 39% nuclear power, which leaves them with a network nearly free of CO_2 emissions. Swiss green energy initiatives are striving to remove nuclear power from the grid (although the referendum has been rejected in national votes) and to cut the nation's energy use by at least 50% by the year 2050.

Switzerland's environmental record is one of the best in the nations of the developed world; the Global Green Economy Index ranks Switzerland among the top 10 green economies worldwide. The people are active recyclers (with 66 to 96 percent of recyclable materials recycled, depending on the canton). It is interesting to note that Switzerland's well-organized recycling system, which utilizes volunteers and railway transport, began in 1865 with the building of the first modern paper manufacturing plant in Biberest. Illegal disposal of garbage in Switzerland is met with heavy fines.

Culture, Media, and Entertainment

The constitution of Switzerland guarantees the freedom of the press and the right to free expression. Switzerland's cultural diversity and multiple national languages, plus its early advances in the availability of printing, account in some part for the fact that historically the country has had the greatest number of newspapers published in proportion to the population's size. News is produced around the clock by the Swiss News Agency (SNA) in three of the country's four languages. The Swiss Broadcasting company (recently renamed as the SRG SSR) oversees television and radio programming but cable networks provide most of Switzerland with access to foreign programming.

Early Swiss literature is mostly German, and it was not until the 18th Century that French became fashionable enough to enter the literary market. Switzerland boasts several German and French speaking authors known worldwide; their Italian and Romansch authors are more modestly popular. Of course, most adults of a certain age remember reading the incredibly popular children's classic novel *Heidi*, by Johanna Spyri, the tale of a Swiss mountain girl who strives to be reunited with her grandfather. Swiss poet Carl Spitteler won the 1919 Nobel Prize in Literature for his contributions to poetry; his masterpiece work is *Olympian Spring*.

Because of the three major cultures that combined to make Switzerland, the resulting Swiss culture is notable for its very diversity, and the Swiss have a wide range of customs. Swiss cooking, just for example, is varied over the cantons, with each developing its own individual traditional dishes. Folk art is diligently practiced and kept alive by organizations devoted to it, through wood carving, embroidery, yodeling and dancing, accompanied and the undeniably Swiss musical instruments of the alphorn and the accordion.

About 1000 museums are spread throughout the country. Important cultural festivals are held annually including the Paléo Festival (a rock-and-roll concert), the Lucerne Festival (featuring classical music), the Montreux Jazz Festival, the Locarno International Film Festival and the Art Basel (and international art fair with showings also in Miami and Hong Kong.

The Romansch culture is somewhat culturally and linguistically isolated, and with the increasing pressures of globalization is struggling to maintain its unusual cultural identity.

SPORTS

It comes as little surprise that mountaineering, skiing, and snowboarding are extremely popular in Switzerland, seeing as the terrain for such sports is ideal. Both the residents of Switzerland and gaggles of tourists gather to play on the Alpine slopes. The Swiss professional football association is the Swiss Super League and Switzerland is home to the highest football pitch in the world: Ottmar Hitzfeld Stadium, 6,600 feet above sea level. Naturally the numerous large and beautiful lakes of Switzerland make it an ideal place for sailing.

The Swiss enjoy watching televised football, skiing, ice hockey, and tennis. Switzerland is the birthplace of Roger Federer, generally considered one of the greatest tennis players of all time.

Though several successful race drivers have come from Switzerland, motorsport racecourses have been banned in Switzerland since 1955's Le Mans disaster, the worst accident in racing history, when debris from a crash flew into the crowd, killing 80 and injuring more than twice that many.

Switzerland has a few traditional sports, including schwingen, a form of traditional wrestling that originated in rural cantons, and which is considered by some to be the national sport. Hornussen is an amusing Swiss variation combining principles of both golf and baseball, and Steinstossen is an ancient game (rather like the stone put) that was played in the Alps from prehistoric times.

LIFE AND TOURISM IN THE ALPS

The Swiss Alps hold the highest mountains of all the Alpine range. The Swiss have built several hydroelectric dams in the Alps and created a fair number of artificial lakes; notably with the effects of global warming reducing the size and runoff of Alpine glaciers, the Swiss are examining alternative solutions and problem solving in their future energy production. The Alps are divided into three "zones":

1. The subalpine zone, located below the tree line, ranging from heights of about 1200-2300 meters depending on which area of the Alps one considers. This is where most towns, people and areas of production are located.

2. The alpine zone, above the treelined, also varies according to location. Some villages can be found here. Below the permafrost limit, which is at about 2600 meters, meadows can be used for grazing.

3. The glacial zone, where snow and ice are permanent. Aside from scientific observatories, no settlements will be found in these areas.

Many of Switzerland's tiny Alpine towns were established in the Middle Ages and continue the traditions of their ancestors, farming hay and grass to feed their cattle through the winter, their cattle supplying the milk for cheese, with each hamlet having its own distinctive flavors of Switzerland's most popular export. The mountain people have an interesting outlook, combining their respect for tradition with the conveniences of modern tech; for example, they must meet guidelines in cheese-production if they want to export the product, but they still follow traditional recipes and techniques.

The towns are too small to warrant official services, and the men are busy working on the farms, so the local housewives serve as the well-trained volunteer fire department, running drills monthly and keeping themselves trained. The towns are made of Alpine wood, and a single fire could be devastating.

Though visitors are made welcome, they should not expect luxuries. The residents of these little towns have no wish to become homes to extravagant mountain lodges. Just for example, the little town of Gimmelwald had itself declared an Avalanche Zone years ago to avoid expansionism. Nearly all these small villages are linked to public transport systems, which are well established in the Alps.

There is one notable exception to their old-fashioned ways: the Swiss farmers supplement their income through the winters by operating nearby lifts and transports that bring tourists into the heights of the Alps. The winter season runs from about November to late May but of course the weather is the final deciding factor on when the season will start and end. Major winter sports destinations include Bernese Oberland, Graubunden and Valais; in many cases tourist towns are traffic-free and only public transportation is available.

The Alps are obviously known for winter sports but in the summertime, the mountains are also set up for enjoyable and manageable hiking and cycling trails. Difficult altitudes are achieved by lifts and cable cars, then miles of paved trails have been established to allow for sightseeing on foot or bicycle. Bike rentals are popular and biking routes well-marked. Because most of the ascents are achieved by car or lift, the bike trails are flat or downhill. The trails are partitioned into manageable lengths and equipped with gondola stations, little cabins that provide food, hot drinks, inexpensive accommodations, so that hikers are not required to carry supplies along with them. The trails are so well-developed that it is possible to hike the Alps from France to Slovenia. Hikers get to meet a good number of friendly, belled cows and goats along the way. Additionally, there are lots of campgrounds, and typical of Switzerland's pride in its cleanliness and amenities, these are well-groomed, with stores and good facilities for the campers.

The traffic-free town of Interlaken is the springboard for multiple ways to view the beauty of the Alps and the surrounding lakes. Some of these options are quite adventurous, including skydiving, paragliding and hang gliding. From Interlaken, one can easily find one's way to the mountain resorts that serve famous Alpine peaks Eiger, Monch and Jungfrau. Trains from Interlaken can take tourists along magnificent mountain views. It is also a well-known destination for backpackers, offering many accommodations specifically for the needs of that brand of tourism.

Mountain climbing is another popular Swiss activity. With more than 250 summits exceeding 3,600 meters, a climber could not ask for more choices in ascents.

Life in Switzerland's Great Cities

The Swiss enjoy the highest per capita income in the world, averaging $88,000 per person, but this privilege comes with one of the highest costs of the living in the world as well. Major urban areas are very expensive places to live. City systems are organized and reliable. The trains and buses run on time in Switzerland – usually down to the second.

The Swiss are hard-working, time-conscious people, but they do not often fall into the traps of overwork. It is more appropriate to say that they "work to live," meaning that they work smarter, not harder, and then thoroughly enjoy their time away from the job. Few businesses remain open during weekends and evenings or have seriously restricted hours. The Swiss take their leisure time as seriously as they take their work. They are proud of their clean cities, streets and rivers and take special care to keep these things pristine.

Generally, the Swiss are quite practical in the way they deal with social problems. For example, when a city is faced with both excessive traffic and rising unemployment, they develop a bike rental system that creates new jobs. In the case of drug abuse, the Swiss government subsidizes safe needles, and public restrooms install blue lights (an interesting trick – it keeps one from being able to find a vein for injection). Drug use is considered a health problem rather than a crime and is dealt with as such.

Most Swiss people live in urban areas (about two-thirds of the population). This is a rather dramatic change that has occurred just over the last century. Before, Switzerland was mostly rural, a country of little Alpine hamlets, mountain herders and plateau farmers. But starting in 1935, urban development took over the Swiss plateau, which has become quite densely populated. Despite some concerns about overcrowding, Swiss cities are renowned for their high quality of life. Swiss cities embrace their clean rivers, with much of the social life occurring on the riverfront, and show great pride are care for their "old town" areas which typically line those same rivers.

Here we'll examine the most populous and famous Swiss cities:

BASEL

Basel is still known for the centuries old and highly acclaimed University of Basel. However, Basel is also the leader of Switzerland's pharmaceutical industry. Novartis and Roche, along with several other drug companies, are headquartered there. Basel's companies are strong players in the life-sciences industries. Basel is often considered a cultural capital of Switzerland, and is home to forty notable museums such as:

» the Kunstmuseum, established in 1661, which was the first publicly accessible art collection in the world
» The Fondation Beyeler, Switzerland's largest art museum
» The Museum of Contemporary Art (Basel), which was the first contemporary art museum in Europe

Basel continues its centuries-old commitment to the promotion of humanism. Basel, Zurich, and Geneva are all rated among the top ten most livable cities in the world.

GENEVA

Like Zurich, Geneva is a global city, though its fame is due more to its international organizations rather than the thrumming business world of Zurich. Known as the Capital of Peace and Freedom, Geneva is home to 35 international organizations and 250 international non-governmental organizations. It is somewhat unusual in that most world cities that host such staggering numbers of international organizations tend to be capital cities, whereas Geneva is not.

Though generally it is known more as a hub humanitarian, political and peace centers, Geneva, too, ranks high as an important financial center on the world stage. Geneva's population is moderate, at slightly over 200,000 persons, and the cost of living there is quite high.

BERN

The unofficial capital, or "Federal City" of Switzerland, is built on a peninsula in the turquoise Aare River. Bern appears stately, but its attitude is laid back and casual. The city is decorated with eleven colorful Renaissance fountains of local heroes and events. One of its most famous sights is the Zytglogge, a medieval clock tower of moving puppets. Bern's city center, many of its medieval buildings still standing, has been designed by UNESCO as a World Heritage Site. In the summer months, citizens love to swim in the river. A popular outing is to hike upstream and then float back to downtown on the current.

Why is Bern considered an "unofficial" capital? Following the inclusion of the final cantons of Valais, Neuchâtel, and Geneva to full membership in 1815, the purposes of a "capital" city for the sake of congressional meetings was given in two-year rotating terms to Lucerne, Zurich and Bern. Eventually Switzerland's Federal Assembly dictated that Bern should function as the Federal City while other important institutions were granted to other cities. As ever, the Swiss believe in compromise. Zurich was given the Federal Polytechnical School, Lucerne the Federal Insurance Court, Lausanne the Federal Supreme Court, and Bellinzona the Federal Criminal Court, just to name a few. Regardless, in the new constitution of 1999, Switzerland did not name a capital or Federal City, and the Swiss Federal Council seems reluctant to pursue the matter; the last measures taken were the formation of a committee to, basically, weigh the pros and cons of such a declaration for Bern – almost twenty years ago.

LAUSANNE

Overlooking Lake Geneva, Lausanne is made up of two sections: the Waterfront and Old City (which is listed in the Inventory of Swiss Heritage Sites). It is often called "The San Francisco of Switzerland" because of the many steep hills throughout the city streets. Lausanne is a mecca for shoppers, with many of the finest and most exclusive shops in the world lining its thoroughfares. It is the smallest city in the world to have a rapid-transit system.

Lausanne has attracted a fair number of writers over the years, both those seeking refuge and those looking for inspiration, including Hemingway, Gibbon, Shelley, and Byron. T.S. Eliot is said to have composed most of *The Waste Land* while in Lausanne).

It is also known as an "international sport" city, hosting about 55 international sports associations in addition to the International Olympic Committee.

LUCERNE

Lucerne is a notably artistic city. The beautiful Chapel Bridge (the oldest covered bridge in Europe) crosses the Ruess, and inside the bridge one can find a series of paintings depicting three centuries of events from Lucerne's history. Swans live on Lake Lucerne. The dam there controls the level of the lake to avoid flooding in the surrounding towns, and little steamer boats take people back and forth to the various lakeside villages. It is within sight of Mounts Pilatus and Rigi and therefore a popular destination for tourism.

Each year near winter's end, a carnival called Fasnacht breaks out in the Old Town streets. It is comparable to Mardi Gras (also having a basis in Catholicism), and is full of costumed characters, parades, indoor parties, and dances, singing and music. The event lasts almost a week and draws tens of thousands of visitors.

ZURICH

The world city of Zurich dates back Roman times, and in Old Town Zurich, some buildings date back to the 12th Century. But by the 19th Century it was a major economic center. Despite its size and financial power, Zurich has surprisingly few tall buildings – many of its districts maintain height restrictions on the buildings.

A major transportation hub for roads, air traffic (its airport serving 60 passenger airlines from around the world) and railways, Zurich is the center from which almost 3,000 trains a day take almost half a million people all over Europe. The largest city in Switzerland, Zurich is home to 1.5 million people and more than 150,000 companies. The people are known for their wealth and for working hard to get it. The city's employees are highly motivated and show a low level of absenteeism. Zurich promotes professional training and education and produces skilled labor at every level. It is ranked as the city with the highest quality of living in the world, but also as the most expensive city in the world.

Hard workers they may be, the people of Zurich are also invested heavily in the arts, classical and contemporary music, opera, theaters, and ballet, combining a respect for tradition with curiosity about new innovations, therefore pushing the envelope to find new forms of expression in these artistic arenas. A couple of interesting Zurich attractions are Europe's oldest vegetarian restaurant, Hiltl, which serves an incredible variety of vegetarian entrees smorgasbord-style. One can also visit the Beyer Clock and Watch Museum, an amazing display of timepieces from 1400 BC to the present.

CONCLUSION

Switzerland's climate, geography and location have determined its position – pardon the pun – in the events of the world. However, it is the fierce resilience of the proud Swiss people that have made it the world power and mediator that it is today. The Swiss are willing to sacrifice, even fight to the death, but show an amazing preference for compromise most of the time, believing in unification and consensus if possible.

Neutrality is Switzerland's unusual calling card, a position that subjects it both envy and criticism. While the subject of controversy in its historic choices, and the subject of suspicion in terms of its secret bank accounts, Switzerland has no more skeletons in its closet than any other European nation, and in many ways, it pays for, or at least offsets, its indiscretions with concerted efforts toward the betterment of mankind and the planet Earth. Switzerland continues to play a leading role in setting the examples for world peace, humanitarian organizations, and forward-thinking environmental and scientific innovations.

As if this were not sufficient to garner admiration, Switzerland remains one of the most beautiful countries in the world, surrounded by the majesty of its mountain ranges, its landscape flowing with clean rivers, and graced by vast lakes.

Its cities are remarkable and its people unconquerable. The Swiss are justifiably proud of their magnificent homeland.